UNBINDING LOVE

Transformative Steps to Release and Heal

COPYRIGHT

All right reserved no part of the publication maybe reproduced, duplicated in any form or by any mean including photocopying, recording or other electronic or mechanical method without the prior verified permission of the publisher.

Copyright© by Luna Everheart202

Table of Contents

CHAPTER ONE

Understanding the Need for Release: Recognizing When Love Requires Letting Go

Figuring out the Requirement for Delivery: Perceiving When Love Requires Giving up Love is many times depicted as a power that ties individuals together, making profound associations and tough bonds. Nonetheless, there are times when love turns into a weight as opposed to a wellspring of satisfaction and backing. In these occurrences, perceiving the requirement for discharge becomes fundamental for self-awareness and close to home prosperity. Love, in its most genuine structure, ought to elevate and enhance our lives. It ought to give us joy, satisfaction, and a feeling of having a place. However, there are circumstances where love turns poisonous, smothering individual development and actually hurting more than great. Perceiving when love requires giving up is a complex and frequently difficult cycle, however it is an urgent step towards recovering one's independence and discovering a sense of reconciliation. One of the key pointers that adoration might should be delivered is the point at which it starts to cause more agony than delight. In sound connections, conflicts and clashes are unavoidable, however they are normally settled through open correspondence and split the difference. Nonetheless, when love turns poisonous, clashes might grow into pernicious contentions, close to home control, or even maltreatment. At the point when the negative parts of a relationship offset the positive ones, it very well might be an indication that the time has come to give up. Another sign that adoration requires giving up is the point at which it thwarts self-improvement and satisfaction. Love ought to rouse us to turn into our best selves, supporting our fantasies and desires. However, now and again, love can become choking, keeping us away from chasing after our objectives and smothering our distinction. Whether an accomplice deters our desires or a relationship that consumes the entirety of our significant investment, perceiving when love is repressing our self-awareness is fundamental for our drawn-out bliss and satisfaction. Furthermore, when love becomes uneven or unreciprocated, it could be an ideal opportunity to give up. Connections flourish with common regard, understanding, and correspondence. At the point when one individual is reliably giving more than they are getting, it makes an unevenness that can prompt hatred and disappointment. Whether lonely love or an accomplice won't meet our feelings, clutching a relationship that isn't commonly satisfying just drags out our torment and keeps us from finding an adoration that is really corresponding. Moreover, when love becomes interwoven with reliance or codependency, it tends to be unfavorable to our prosperity. Reliance in a relationship happens when one individual depends on the other for their healthy identity worth, approval, or close to home steadiness. Codependency makes this reliance a stride further, with the two accomplices empowering each other's unfortunate ways of behaving and depending on the relationship to satisfy their feelings. In the two cases, the relationship turns into a brace as opposed to a wellspring of help, and giving up becomes essential for the two players to recover their independence and close to home freedom. It's vital to take note of that perceiving the requirement for discharge doesn't lessen the affection that once existed in the relationship. Love is an intricate and diverse feeling that can get through in any event, when the actual relationship is presently not suitable. Relinquishing somebody we love doesn't imply that we quit really focusing on them or that our sentiments were not veritable. All things considered, it implies recognizing that the relationship is done serving our most elevated great and deciding to focus on our own prosperity and satisfaction. All in all, understanding the requirement for discharge is fundamental for perceiving when love requires giving up. Whether this is on the grounds that the relationship has become poisonous, frustrating self-awareness, unreciprocated, or described by reliance, perceiving when now is the right time to give up is critical for our profound prosperity and self-improvement. Relinquishing somebody we love is rarely simple, however it is many times important for our drawn-out bliss and satisfaction

Embracing Acknowledgment: Reaching Terms with the Finish of a

Relationship Acknowledgment is a significant and frequently testing process, particularly when it includes the determination of a relationship. Whether the closure was expected or unforeseen, exploring the intricacies of giving up and embracing acknowledgment requires persistence, thoughtfulness, and strength. In this investigation, we dig into the multi-layered excursion of reaching terms with the termination of a friendship, figuring out its close to home scene, and tracking down the way towards recuperating and development.

1. Recognizing Reality: The most important move towards embracing acknowledgment is recognizing the truth. This includes confronting the reality of the relationship's end

without refusal or opposition. It requires a readiness to face awkward feelings and acknowledge that the elements of the relationship have changed irreversibly.

2. Permitting Pain to Unfold: Sadness is a characteristic reaction to misfortune, and permitting oneself to experience and communicate it is fundamental for recuperating. Reaching terms with the termination of a friendship frequently includes grieving the deficiency of the organization as well as the fantasies, expectations, and assumptions related with it. It's critical to allow oneself to lament completely and to respect the feelings that emerge during this cycle.

3. Embracing Vulnerability: Acknowledgment requires weakness

— the eagerness to free oneself up to the torment and uneasiness that go with the conclusion of a friendship. It includes recognizing one's own weaknesses and permitting oneself to be seen and upheld by others during this difficult time. Embracing weakness cultivates association and works with the recuperating system.

4. Relinquishing Control: One of the most moving parts of reaching terms with the conclusion of a friendship is giving up control. It's normal to need to clutch what was natural and unsurprising, yet sticking to the past just draws out the agony and hinders development. Acknowledgment includes giving up to the vulnerability representing things to come and confiding during the time spent recuperating and change.

5. Finding Significance in the Pain: While the termination of a friendship can be significantly difficult, it likewise offers a chance for development and self-revelation. Embracing acknowledgment implies rethinking the experience as a chance for learning and self-improvement. It includes tracking down importance in the torment and involving it as an impetus for positive change.

6. Rehearsing Self-Compassion: Self-sympathy is a significant part of embracing acknowledgment. It includes treating oneself with graciousness, understanding, and non-judgment during seasons of affliction. Rather than taking part in self-fault or analysis, rehearsing self-sympathy implies offering oneself the very compassion and backing that

one would propose to a dear companion.

7. Developing Gratitude: Even in the midst of the aggravation of a relationship's end, there are many times snapshots of appreciation to be found. Embracing acknowledgment includes developing appreciation for the encounters, illustrations, and recollections imparted to an accomplice, regardless of whether the relationship at last reaches a conclusion. Appreciation encourages a feeling of viewpoint and assists shift with centering from misfortune to appreciation.

8. Looking for Support: Reaching terms with the conclusion of a friendship isn't an excursion that ought to be embraced alone. Looking for help from companions, family, or

a specialist can give priceless direction, approval, and viewpoint during this difficult time. Encircling oneself with a strong organization can offer solace and strength as one explores the intricacies of acknowledgment.

9. Recovering Independence: A relationship's end can frequently leave people feeling uncontrolled and unsure of their character beyond the organization. Embracing acknowledgment includes recovering autonomy and rediscovering one's identity beyond the relationship. It's a chance to investigate individual interests, objectives, and interests and to develop areas of strength for an of independence.

10. Embracing Another Beginning: At last, embracing acknowledgment

is tied in with embracing the chance of a fresh start. It's tied in with recognizing that the termination of a friendship isn't the finish of one's story yet rather the start of another part. It's tied in with embracing the obscure with fortitude and good faith, believing that mending and development are conceivable even despite significant misfortune. All in all, reaching terms with the termination of a friendship is a profoundly private and extraordinary excursion. It requires fortitude, weakness, and self-sympathy to explore the intricacies of acknowledgment. By recognizing reality, permitting misery to unfurl, embracing weakness, relinquishing control, tracking down significance in the torment, rehearsing self-sympathy, developing appreciation, looking for help, recovering freedom, and embracing a fresh start, people can set out on an excursion of recuperating and development that at last prompts acknowledgment and restoration.

CHAPTER THREE

Regarding Feelings: Exploring Misery, Misfortune, and Recuperating In the wake of Giving up Relinquishing somebody we love can be quite possibly of the most difficult involvement with life. Whether it's the conclusion of a heartfelt friendship, the departure of a kinship, or the death of a friend or family member, the excursion of exploring distress, misfortune, and recuperating is profoundly private and complex. In this investigation, we dive into the multifaceted course of regarding feelings in the wake of giving up, grasping the phases of misery, and embracing the way to mending. Pain is a characteristic reaction to misfortune, including a scope of feelings like bitterness, outrage, disavowal, haggling, and in the long run acknowledgment. Every individual's insight of pain is novel, impacted by variables like the idea of the misfortune, individual survival techniques, and emotionally supportive networks. Exploring melancholy includes recognizing and respecting these feelings, permitting oneself to feel and communicate them without judgment or concealment. The most important phase in exploring anguish is frequently recognizing the truth of the misfortune. Whether it's the conclusion of a friendship or the demise of a friend or family member, tolerating the reality of the matter is essential in starting the lamenting system. Disavowal and skepticism may at first safeguard us from the full effect of the misfortune, yet embracing the truth is fundamental for pushing ahead on the way to mending. As we defy the truth of the misfortune, we might wind up submerged in a tornado of feelings. Misery, maybe the most conspicuous inclination related with distress, can feel overpowering and widely inclusive. It's essential to permit ourselves to completely experience and express our trouble, whether through tears, journaling, or looking for help from friends and family. Smothering bitterness can delay the lamenting system and repress mending. Close by trouble, outrage is one more typical inclination experienced during despondency. Whether coordinated towards the individual we've lost, ourselves, or outer conditions, outrage is a characteristic reaction to sensations of foul play or weakness. While it's not unexpected to feel furious, it's vital for track down solid source for communicating and handling this inclination, like actual work, imaginative outlets, or treatment. Notwithstanding misery and outrage, sorrow may likewise appear as sensations of culpability, lament, or even alleviation. Culpability frequently emerges from addressing past activities or choices and can weigh vigorously on our brains and hearts. It's essential to perceive that we are just human and to rehearse self-empathy despite culpability. Likewise, liberating sensation, especially with regards to a difficult or turbulent relationship, are normal and don't decrease the legitimacy of our despondency. Exploring melancholy likewise includes recognizing the influxes of feeling that travel every which way capriciously. Distress is definitely not a direct cycle but instead a progression of ups and downs, back and forth movements. Occasionally might feel simpler than others, while others might bring overpowering pity or outrage. It's essential to permit ourselves the space and elegance to ride these profound waves without judgment or assumption. Close by respecting our own feelings, looking for help from others can be significant in exploring sadness. Whether it's companions, relatives, or a specialist, having an emotionally supportive network to rest on can give solace, approval, and viewpoint during testing times. Discussing our thoughts and encounters with others can assist us with feeling less alone in our sorrow and advise us that we are upheld and cherished. As well as looking for help from others, taking part in taking care of oneself practices can help support and feed us as we explore misery. This might include focusing on exercises that give us pleasure and solace, like investing energy in nature, rehearsing care or contemplation, or taking part in imaginative pursuits. Dealing with our physical, close to home, and otherworldly prosperity is fundamental for mending and flexibility. As we venture through the lamenting system, we may continuously end up moving towards acknowledgment and recuperating. Acknowledgment doesn't mean neglecting or limiting the meaning of the misfortune yet rather finding a sense of peace with it and coordinating it into our lives in a significant manner. Recuperating isn't tied in with eradicating the aggravation of misfortune yet rather figuring out how to live with it and tracking down importance and development amidst it. All in all, exploring melancholy, misfortune, and mending in the wake of giving up is a profoundly private and groundbreaking excursion. By regarding our feelings, looking for help from others, and taking part in taking care of oneself practices, we can explore the intricacies of distress with boldness, versatility, and beauty. Yet again however the street might be testing, it is through respecting our feelings and embracing the method involved with mending that we can at last discover a sense of harmony and completeness.

CHAPTER FOUR

Developing Self-Sympathy: Offering Consideration and Understanding to Yourself In the meantime --- Self-sympathy, frequently ignored in the midst of close to home pain, is a fundamental part of recuperating and development, particularly while relinquishing somebody you love. It envelops the capacity to treat oneself with consideration, understanding, and absolution during testing times. In the excursion of unbinding love, developing self-empathy turns into an extraordinary step towards delivery and mending.

Figuring out Self-Empathy Self-empathy includes three key components: self-generosity, normal humankind, and care, as proposed by Dr. Kristin Neff, a spearheading specialist in this field. Self-thoughtfulness involves being delicate and understanding toward oneself as opposed to brutally self-basic. Normal mankind underlines perceiving that misery and difficulties are important for the human experience, cultivating a feeling of association instead of disconnection. Care includes monitoring one's contemplations and feelings without judgment.

Embracing Self-Generosity While relinquishing somebody you love, it's generally expected to encounter self-fault, culpability, or sensations of shamefulness. In any case, self-generosity empowers a change in context, permitting oneself to recognize these sentiments without judgment. Rather than castigating oneself for previous slip-ups or weaknesses, rehearsing self-graciousness includes treating oneself with a similar sympathy and compassion one would propose to a dear companion experiencing the same thing. Self-thoughtfulness can appear through different taking care of oneself practices, for example, participating in exercises that give pleasure, looking for help from friends and family, or just permitting oneself to rest and re-energize. These demonstrations of self-supporting build up the possibility that you are meriting adoration and sympathy, even in the midst of profound torment.

Perceiving Normal Humankind In the midst of sorrow, it's not difficult to feel alone in your battles, accepting that no other person might actually grasp the profundity of your aggravation. In any case, embracing the idea of normal mankind advises us that enduring is an intrinsic piece of the human condition. Incalculable people have encountered the throb of giving up and the excursion of mending that follows. By perceiving that your encounters are shared by others, you develop a feeling of association and having a place. This acknowledgment can reduce sensations of disengagement and self-judgment, offering comfort in the comprehension that you are in good company in your excursion.

Rehearsing Care Care assumes a vital part in self-sympathy by permitting you to notice your considerations and feelings with non-critical mindfulness. When confronted with the strife of giving up, it's normal for the brain to winding into rumination or self-analysis. Be that as it may, care urges you to notice these considerations without getting ensnared in them. Care rehearses, like contemplation or profound breathing activities, give a space to thoughtfulness and self-reflection. By developing present-second mindfulness, you can move toward your feelings with interest and receptiveness, cultivating a more prominent feeling of clearness and acknowledgment.

Defeating Self-Analysis frequently turns into an obstruction to self-empathy, as the inward voice of judgment sabotages one's feeling of value and deservingness of adoration. Nonetheless, testing self-analysis requires a change in context, reevaluating negative self-talk with self-merciful language. Rather than criticizing yourself for previous slip-ups or saw insufficiencies, work on addressing yourself with benevolence and understanding. Supplant cruel self-analysis with uplifting statements and backing, recognizing your intrinsic worth and mankind.

Excusing Yourself Relinquishing somebody you love frequently includes excusing yourself for any apparent bad behaviors or second thoughts. Self-pardoning is a significant demonstration of self-sympathy, delivering the weight of culpability or disgrace that weighs weighty on the heart. To develop self-pardoning, recognizing the humankind of your missteps and imperfections is fundamental. Comprehend that you are innately defective, very much like every other person, and that errors are valuable open doors for development and learning. By stretching out absolution to yourself, you free yourself from the chains of self-fault and make the way for mending and change.

Looking for Help In snapshots of personal strife, looking for help from others can be instrumental in encouraging self-empathy. Whether from companions, family, or a specialist, having a steady organization can give approval, compassion, and consolation during troublesome times. Contact believed people who can offer a listening ear, a shoulder to rest on, or functional counsel. Permit yourself to be defenseless and request help while required, perceiving that getting support is definitely not an indication of shortcoming however a demonstration of your boldness and strength.

   Embracing Defect, A piece of self-empathy includes embracing your inborn flaws and weaknesses. Relinquishing somebody you love can inspire deep-seated insecurities or disappointment, as you wrestle with the temporariness of connections. In any case, embracing defect recognizes that life is untidy and erratic, and that development frequently emerges from difficulty. Rather than making progress toward unreachable goals of flawlessness, practice self-acknowledgment and confidence notwithstanding your imperfections and inadequacies. Perceive that your value isn't dependent upon outside approval or accomplishments, however comes from your inborn mankind and uniqueness.

Observing Versatility As you explore the excursion of unbinding love and developing self-sympathy, praise your versatility and strength en route. In spite of the aggravation and grief, you have persevered and continued on, exhibiting the surprising limit of the human soul to recuperate and develop. Recognize the boldness it takes to face your weaknesses and embrace the method involved with giving up. Commend every little triumph and achievement, perceiving that mending is a nonlinear excursion loaded up with highs and lows.

Embracing Self-Empathy as a Deep-rooted Practice At last, developing self-empathy isn't an objective however a deep-rooted venture. As you keep on exploring the intricacies of life and love, make sure to treat yourself with benevolence, understanding, and absolution en route. Embrace self-sympathy as a core value in your communications with yourself as well as other people, cultivating a feeling of association, compassion, and flexibility. By offering yourself a similar sympathy and care you would propose to a treasured companion, you prepare for recuperating, development, and change in the excursion of unbinding love.

Delivering Connections: Confining from Assumptions and Recollections to Discover a sense of reconciliation in the excursion of life, connections to assumptions and recollections frequently mesh themselves into the texture of our reality. They shape our insights, impact our choices, and variety our encounters. Nonetheless, as we explore the intricacies of connections and the steadily changing scenes of life, there comes while delivering these connections becomes fundamental for our prosperity and internal harmony. To genuinely comprehend the method involved with delivering connections, it's significant to dive into its complexities. We should investigate this extraordinary excursion bit by bit. First and foremost, what are connections? Connections are the close to home bonds we structure with individuals, thoughts, or results. They come from our cravings, fears, and previous encounters, interlacing with our personalities and forming our perspective. Assumptions, specifically, emerge from connections to explicit results or ways of behaving. Recollections, then again, are impressions of previous encounters that we clutch, frequently impacting our current discernments and activities. Disconnecting from assumptions and recollections doesn't mean deleting them from our psyches or denying their importance. All things considered, it includes relaxing the grasp they have on us, permitting space for acknowledgment, development, and at last, internal harmony. One of the primaries moves toward delivering connections is developing mindfulness. This includes noticing our contemplations, feelings, and ways of behaving without judgment. Through care practices like contemplation, journaling, or just considering our encounters, we can acquire understanding into the connections that are keeping us down. Mindfulness permits us to perceive when assumptions or recollections are impacting our insights and choices, enabling us to pick an alternate way. Whenever mindfulness is laid out, the subsequent stage is acknowledgment. Acknowledgment doesn't mean renunciation or endorsement of a circumstance; rather, it includes recognizing reality all things considered, without obstruction or connection. This incorporates tolerating that individual may not live up to our assumptions, connections might change, and recollections might summon both bliss and agony. By embracing acknowledgment, we free ourselves from the battle against what is and open ourselves to additional opportunities. With mindfulness and acknowledgment as our aides, we can start the most common way of giving up. Giving up is a demonstration of give up, delivering our connection to explicit results or previous encounters. It requires mental fortitude and weakness as we surrender control and confidence in the progression of life. Giving up doesn't occur at the same time; it's a slow unfurling, a progression of little strides towards freedom. One of the most difficult parts of delivering connections is segregating from assumptions. Assumptions frequently emerge from our cravings and convictions about how things ought to be. Whether it's anticipating that others should act a specific way, taking a stab at flawlessness, or sticking to a dream representing things to come, assumptions can make superfluous enduring when reality doesn't line up with them. Isolating from assumptions includes reevaluating our outlook, moving from connection to results to a mentality of transparency and acknowledgment. It implies embracing the current second with interest and miracle, permitting life to unfurl naturally without attempting to compel it into a foreordained form. Essentially, disengaging from recollections requires an eagerness to relinquish the past and embrace the present. Recollections, particularly those related with huge profound encounters, can hold a strong grasp on our cognizance, impacting our discernments and ways of behaving. While recollections can be appreciated for the illustrations they show us, sticking to them can keep us from completely captivating with the current second. Segregating from recollections includes rethinking our relationship to the past, regarding its importance while perceiving that we are not characterized by it. It implies finding appreciation for the encounters that have molded us and embracing the chance for development and recharging in the present time and place. As we discharge connections to assumptions and recollections, we make space for inward harmony to thrive. Inward harmony isn't the shortfall of difficulties or challenges; rather, it's a condition established in acknowledgment, appreciation, and presence. The quiet emerges when we let go of the need to control or oppose what is and give up to the progression of life. Internal harmony permits us to explore life's highs and lows with effortlessness and versatility, realizing that we are grounded in our actual pith. All in all, delivering connections to assumptions and recollections is a groundbreaking excursion towards inward harmony. By developing mindfulness, acknowledgment, and the eagerness to give up, we free ourselves from the shackles of connection and open ourselves to the excellence and probability of the current second. In doing as such, we find a significant feeling of freedom and discover a sense of reconciliation in the midst of life's consistently evolving tide.

CHAPTER SIX

Defining Limits: Laying out Solid Cutoff points for Your Close to home Prosperity In the multifaceted scene of human connections, defining limits remains as a foundation for keeping up with close to home prosperity. These undetectable lines depict where one individual's independence closes and another's starts, protecting individual space, values, and psychological wellness. While defining limits could appear to be clear, it's a nuanced interaction that requires mindfulness, decisiveness, and sympathy. At its pith, defining limits includes perceiving and imparting our requirements, cutoff points, and inclinations to other people. It's tied in with pushing for ourselves without responsibility or conciliatory sentiment, cultivating better collaborations, and protecting our close to home balance. However, for some, defining limits can incite tension, responsibility, or anxiety toward struggle. Be that as it may, by understanding the importance and methods of limit setting, one can leave on a groundbreaking excursion toward more noteworthy self-esteem and satisfaction. First and foremost, it's pivotal to comprehend the reason why limits are essential. Limits act as defensive safeguards, protecting us from mischief, double-dealing, and profound channel. Without them, we risk overstretching ourselves, undermining our qualities, and exposing ourselves to harmful connections or circumstances. Picture a wall around a nursery: it keeps out undesirable interlopers while supporting what's inside. Essentially, defining limits develops a safe and sustaining climate for self-improvement and prosperity. To lay out solid limits, mindfulness is principal. This includes tuning into our sentiments, distinguishing our cutoff points, and recognizing our requirements and values. Ponder previous encounters where you felt awkward or abused. What were the admonition signs? How could you wish to be dealt with? By perceiving our triggers and weaknesses, we gain knowledge into the limits we want to set to safeguard ourselves. When we comprehend our limits, the subsequent stage is conveying them really. This requires clearness, decisiveness, and regard. Start by communicating your limits straightforwardly and confidently, utilizing "I" explanations to convey your sentiments and requirements without accusing or denouncing others. For example, rather than saying, "You generally cause me to feel remorseful," attempt, "I feel overpowered when I'm continually approached to help without being given time for myself." In addition, supporting limits with steady actions is fundamental. Limits are useless if not maintained, so be ready to emphatically authorize them when essential. This could include expressing no to demands that surpass your cutoff points, leaving impolite collaborations, or enjoying some time off from connections that channel your energy. Keep in mind, defining limits isn't tied in with being egotistical; it's tied in with regarding yourself and encouraging better associations. Moreover, defining limits requires exploring through expected obstruction or pushback. A few people might challenge or negligence your limits, either out of obliviousness or insolence. In such cases, it's vital to stand firm and repeat your limits smoothly and confidently. Be ready for awkward discussions, however recall that focusing on your prosperity isn't self-centered — it's important for your psychological wellness and joy. Moreover, it's critical to perceive those limits can develop over the long run. As we develop, change, and study ourselves, our limits might move to mirror our advancing requirements and values. Along these lines, it's fundamental to routinely rethink and change our limits to guarantee they stay lined up with our close to home prosperity. In defining limits, expanding a similar regard and understanding to others is likewise crucial. Similarly, as we affirm our limits, we should respect those of others, perceiving and regarding their independence and cutoff points. Solid connections blossom with shared regard, correspondence, and split the difference, with the two players effectively tuning in and answering each other's requirements. Besides, defining limits is definitely not a one-time task yet a continuous practice. It requires mindfulness, boldness, and obligation to focus on our prosperity reliably. It's normal to experience difficulties or difficulties en route, however each experience offers a chance for development and learning.

Be patient and humane with yourself as you explore this excursion, commending your advancement and versatility. All in all, defining limits is a crucial expertise for protecting our close to home prosperity and cultivating better connections. By understanding our requirements, conveying self-assuredly, and supporting limits with predictable activities, we make a defensive safeguard that permits us to explore existence with more noteworthy certainty and flexibility. Embrace the groundbreaking force of limit setting and leave on an excursion toward more noteworthy dignity, satisfaction, and inward harmony.

Tracking down Help: Looking for Direction from Companions, Family, or Restorative Assets Introduction: In the excursion of unbinding love, finding support turns into a fundamental mainstay of solidarity. When confronted with the overwhelming errand of delivering a friend or family member and leaving on a mending venture, looking for direction from different sources can give priceless help. Whether it's from companions, relatives, or remedial assets, the encouraging group of people assumes an essential part in exploring the intricacies of profound mending and change. Significance of Help: At the beginning, it's essential to comprehend the reason why looking for help is significant during the time spent delivering and mending from a past affection. While encountering shock or the termination of a friendship, people frequently end up wrecked by a scope of feelings - from trouble and pain to outrage and disarray. In such fierce times, having an emotionally supportive network can offer a place of refuge for articulation, approval, and understanding. Companions: A Help of Understanding and Compassion Companions are much of the time the primary line of help for some people exploring the result of a separation or the conclusion of a heartfelt friendship. Genuine companions offer a listening ear, a shoulder to rest on, and resolute sympathy during seasons of misery. They give a feeling of having a place and association, advising us that we're in good company in our battles. Companions assume an essential part in approving our feelings and encounters. By sharing their own accounts of sorrow and mending, they assist us with feeling comprehended and less disconnected in our torment. Additionally, companions offer down to earth help, whether it's through straightforward signals like getting to know one another or offering help with day-to-day undertakings. Family: The Groundwork of Unqualified Love and Soundness Relatives, as well, structure a fundamental piece of our emotionally supportive network during seasons of inner commotion. Dissimilar to fellowships, family bonds are in many cases established in well-established love and shared history, making them a wellspring of solace and steadiness during turbulent times. Relatives give a special type of help portrayed by unqualified love and acknowledgment. They offer a place of refuge where we can communicate our rawest feelings unafraid of judgment. Whether it's a parent offering consoling hug or kin giving a listening ear, family backing can be significantly soothing and consoling. Helpful Assets: Proficient Direction and Recuperating Modalities Notwithstanding support from loved ones, looking for direction from remedial assets can be gigantically advantageous during the time spent delivering and mending from past affection. Specialists, instructors, and care groups offer an organized climate where people can investigate their sentiments, gain bits of knowledge, and pick up survival techniques. Treatment gives a non-critical space to self-investigation and reflection. A prepared specialist can assist people with unwinding complex feelings, distinguish fundamental examples, and foster sound survival techniques. Through strategies like mental conduct treatment (CBT), care, and relational treatment, people can acquire a more profound comprehension of themselves and their connections. Support bunches likewise offer a feeling of local area and fortitude. Interfacing with other people who have encountered comparable difficulties can cultivate a feeling of having a place and approval. Bunch treatment meetings give amazing chances to shared encounters, common help, and aggregate mending. Conclusion: In the excursion of unbinding love, looking for help from companions, family, and remedial assets is certainly not an indication of shortcoming however of solidarity. These mainstays of help offer sympathy, approval, and direction during seasons of inner disturbance. Whether it's through ardent discussions with companions, the unflinching affection for relatives, or the expert direction of advisors, finding support is fundamental for mending and change. By connecting and permitting ourselves to be upheld, we can explore the difficulties of delivering past adoration and leave on an excursion of mending and recharging.

Rediscovering Yourself: Reconnecting with Individual Interests, Objectives, and Character

Introduction: Rediscovering oneself is an unpredictable excursion that frequently starts with reflection and mindfulness. When confronted with the need to relinquish a huge relationship, whether heartfelt etc., people might find themselves loose, uncertain of what their identity is or what they need. In such occasions, reconnecting with individual interests, objectives, and personality becomes vital for recuperating and development. This paper investigates the groundbreaking advances engaged with this cycle, featuring the significance of self-investigation, reconsideration of needs, and the quest for credibility. Figuring out Private Interests: Interests are the fuel that lights the spirit, driving people towards satisfaction and reason. Notwithstanding, amidst a relationship, these interests might assume a lower priority as one puts investment into sustaining the association. Rediscovering oneself includes reigniting these flares, diving into exercises and interests that once given pleasure and energy. Whether it's painting, composing, climbing, or cooking, reconnecting with individual interests permits people to recover a feeling of personality free of their past connections. Reconnecting with Objectives: Objectives act as directing lights, forming our way of living and giving an internal compass. However, when entwined with the desires of an accomplice, these objectives might become obscured or failed to remember by and large. Rediscovering oneself involves returning to these goals, assessing whether they actually impact one's qualities and wants. This might include defining new objectives or committing once again to old ones, adjusting them to self-improvement and satisfaction. Whether it's progressing in a profession, venturing to the far corners of the planet, or mastering another expertise, chasing after objectives cultivates a feeling of direction and organization in one's life.

Investigating Character: Character is diverse, enveloping different viewpoints like qualities, convictions, and character attributes. Be that as it may, with regards to a relationship, people may subliminally form themselves to fit the assumptions for their accomplice, failing to focus on their true selves. Rediscovering oneself requires stripping back these layers, analyzing the center parts of one's personality with interest and self-sympathy. This cycle might include addressing long-held convictions, defying instabilities, and embracing parts of oneself that have been disregarded or stifled. By embracing genuineness and embracing all features of their personality, people can develop a more profound identity mindfulness and acknowledgment.

The Significance of Self-Investigation: Self-investigation is the foundation of rediscovery, furnishing people with the space to reflect, introspect, and develop. This might appear as journaling, contemplation, or participating in treatment, permitting people to dig underneath the surface and uncover their actual cravings and inspirations. Through self-investigation, people can recognize examples of conduct, gain knowledge into their profound scene, and foster a more profound comprehension of themselves. This cycle is fundamental for shedding the layers of molding and cultural assumptions, preparing for real self-articulation and satisfaction.

Reexamining Needs: Relinquishing a relationship frequently prompts people to reevaluate their needs and values. What once appeared to be significant may never again hold a similar importance, as people realign their concentration towards the main thing to them. This might include reprioritizing connections, vocation desires, or way of life decisions, putting more noteworthy accentuation on self-improvement and prosperity. By reexamining needs, people can make a day-to-day existence that is more lined up with their credible selves, cultivating a feeling of satisfaction and happiness.

Developing Self-Sympathy: Rediscovering oneself can be a difficult and on occasion, excruciating interaction. It expects people to defy their feelings of dread, uncertainties, and past injuries with generosity and understanding.

Developing self-sympathy includes treating oneself with a similar warmth and compassion as one would a dear companion, recognizing that flaw is essential for the human experience. This implies embracing weakness, permitting oneself to feel feelings without judgment, and offering mercy for previous oversights. Through self-empathy, people can explore the highs and lows of self-revelation with flexibility and effortlessness. Looking for Help: Self-disclosure isn't an excursion that one should leave on alone. Looking for help from companions, family, or a specialist can give important direction and support en route. Whether it's sharing encounters, looking for counsel, or just having a listening ear, encouraging groups of people offer a feeling of having a place and approval that is fundamental for development. Furthermore, encircling oneself with people who elevate and move can cultivate a positive climate helpful for self-investigation and self-awareness.

 Embracing Legitimacy: At its center, rediscovering oneself is tied in with embracing realness and living in arrangement with one's actual self. This implies relinquishing cultural assumptions, social standards, and the requirement for outer approval, and on second thought, following the internal compass of one's heart. Validness breeds certainty, strength, and a profound feeling of satisfaction, as people honor their one-of-a-kind gifts and interests without conciliatory sentiment. By embracing genuineness, people can live with aim and reason, making a day-to-day existence that is wealthy in significance and euphoria.

Rediscovering oneself is an excursion of self-revelation, development, and change. By reconnecting with individual interests, objectives, and personality, people can explore the most common way of giving up with beauty and strength. Through self-investigation, reexamination of needs, and the quest for genuineness, people can rise up out of the cinders of a past relationship more grounded, savvier, and more enabled than any time in recent memory. In embracing their actual selves, they track down recuperating and freedom as well as a

restored feeling of direction and
probability.

Rehearsing Absolution: Relinquishing Hatred and Tracking down Closure Pardoning is a significant demonstration that can free the essence from the weights of disdain and outrage. A groundbreaking interaction permits people to deliver the grasp of gloomy feelings, track down conclusion, and leave on an excursion of mending and internal harmony. In this investigation, we dig into the profundities of pardoning, grasping its quintessence, benefits, and pragmatic moves toward develop it in our lives.

Grasping Forgiveness At its center, pardoning is a cognizant choice to deliver sensations of disdain, outrage, or retribution towards somebody who has violated us. It doesn't approve or legitimize the atrocities yet rather looks to liberate the forgiver from the profound shackles that tight spot them. Pardoning isn't tied in with neglecting or pardoning the bad behavior yet about relinquishing the close to home connection to the aggravation it caused.

The Quintessence of Forgiveness Pardoning is a multi-layered idea that envelops different parts of profound, mental, and otherworldly mending. It includes sympathy, compassion, and understanding towards oneself as well as other people. By excusing, people recognize their own mankind and the humankind of the individuals who have truly hurt them. It is a significant demonstration of confidence and self-sympathy, perceiving that clutching disdain just sustains languishing.

The Advantages of Forgiveness The act of pardoning yields various advantages for both the forgiver and the excused. For the forgiver, it offers profound freedom, delivering repressed outrage and sharpness that can weigh intensely on the heart and brain. It lessens pressure, uneasiness, and misery, advancing in general prosperity and emotional well-being. Pardoning encourages better connections, as it permits people to relinquish feelings of spite and develop sympathy and understanding towards others. For the pardoned, absolution can be extraordinary too. It offers the chance for reclamation and compromise, reestablishing harmed connections and encouraging recuperating and development. It permits people to break liberated from the pattern of responsibility and disgrace, preparing for individual change and recharging.

Reasonable Moves toward Develop Forgiveness Developing absolution requires expectation, tolerance, and practice. A continuous cycle unfurls after some time, expecting people to take part in self-reflection, sympathy, and empathy towards themselves as well as other people. Here is a reasonable move toward cultivate pardoning in your life:

1. Recognize the Hurt : Start by recognizing the aggravation and hurt

brought about by the bad behavior.
Permit yourself to feel the feelings
that emerge without judgment or
concealment.

2. Figure out the Point of view of
the Offender : Attempt to grasp the
intentions, conditions, and encounters
that might have driven the guilty
party to act the manner in which they
did. Sympathy and empathy can
assist with relaxing sensations of
hatred and outrage.

3. Discharge Pessimistic Emotions :
Practice profound delivery strategies,
for example, journaling, reflection, or
treatment to process and delivery
gloomy feelings. Permit yourself to
relinquish outrage, hatred, and
harshness.

4. Develop Empathy : Cultivate compassion towards yourself as well as other people by perceiving the common mankind and weakness that ties all of us. Comprehend that no one's perfect and merits sympathy and understanding.

5. Set Boundaries : While absolution is significant, it is likewise vital for defined solid limits to shield yourself from additional mischief. Convey your requirements and assumptions plainly and decisively.

6. Practice Self-Compassion : Be delicate and kind to yourself all through the absolution interaction. Practice taking care of oneself, self-sympathy, and self-pardoning as you explore the intricacies of mending.

7. Pick Forgiveness : At last, pardoning is a decision. Decide to deliver sensations of hatred and outrage, and embrace pardoning as a pathway to mending and freedom. Tracking down Conclusion Through Forgiveness Pardoning is an amazing asset for tracking down conclusion and pushing ahead from past damages. It permits people to deliver the grasp of the past and embrace the present with a feeling of harmony and acknowledgment. Conclusion doesn't be guaranteed to mean neglecting or deleting the past but instead wiping the slate clean with it and permitting oneself to push ahead unburdened by outrage and hatred. All in all, pardoning is an extraordinary cycle that offers freedom, mending, and reestablishment. By rehearsing

absolution, people can deliver the shackles of disdain and track down conclusion and inward harmony. It is a significant demonstration of confidence, empathy, and humankind that has the ability to change connections and lives. As we leave on the excursion of absolution, may we find comfort in the force of giving up and embrace the opportunity that pardoning brings

CHAPTER TEN

Embracing Development: Perceiving the Extraordinary Force of Giving up and Pushing Ahead Introduction: In the embroidered artwork of human encounters, scarcely any cycles are basically as significant and testing as giving up. Whether it's saying goodbye to an esteemed relationship, delivering an unfulfilled dream, or surrendering a long-held conviction, the demonstration of giving up is both a workmanship and a need for self-awareness. In this investigation, we dive into the groundbreaking force of giving up, figuring out its subtleties, and embracing the way ahead with receptiveness and fortitude.

Understanding the Idea of Giving up: At its center, giving up includes delivering connection to results or people. A cycle requires reflection, acknowledgment, and frequently, significant close to home work. Giving up doesn't suggest neglecting or denying the meaning of what's being delivered; rather, it's tied in with recognizing its place in our lives and deciding to push ahead notwithstanding its nonattendance.

Perceiving the Requirement for Delivery: The choice to give up frequently emerges from an acknowledgment that hanging on no longer serves our most elevated great. Whether a harmful relationship smothers our development or a profession way that no longer lines up with our interests, there comes a second when we understand that sticking to the natural just frustrates our advancement. Embracing Acknowledgment: Acknowledgment is a foundation of the giving up process. It includes recognizing reality all things considered, without obstruction or judgment. Acknowledgment doesn't infer endorsement of the circumstance yet rather a readiness to stand up to it with clearness and poise. By tolerating what can't be transformed, we free ourselves from the weight of vain obstruction and make the way for change. Exploring Distress and Misfortune: Giving up frequently involves a time of grieving for what used to be or what could have been. Melancholy is a characteristic reaction to misfortune, whether it's the departure of a friend or family member, a relationship, or a fantasy. It's fundamental for honor our feelings during this time, permitting ourselves to sympathize with profoundly and express our agony in sound ways. Through distress, we recuperate, and through mending, we track down the solidarity to push ahead. Developing Self-Sympathy: Giving up can be a profoundly weak interaction, laden with self-uncertainty and self-analysis. Developing self-empathy is fundamental during this time, offering ourselves similar consideration and understanding we would stretch out to a dear companion. Self-empathy includes embracing our blemishes, recognizing our mankind, and treating ourselves with tenderness and care.

Delivering Connections: Connections are the strings that tight spot us to the past, keeping us from completely embracing the current second. Relinquishing connections includes slackening our hold on assumptions, recollections, and wants. It's tied in with giving up the requirement for control and permitting life to unfurl naturally, confiding in the insight of the universe.

Defining Limits: Limits are fundamental for protecting our close to home prosperity as we explore the giving up process. Defining limits includes characterizing what is and isn't satisfactory in that frame of mind with others and ourselves. Limits shield us from control, double-dealing, and close to home mischief, permitting us to focus on our requirements and values.

Tracking down Help: Giving up can feel like a single excursion, however it's memorable fundamental that we don't need to walk this way alone. Tracking down help from companions, family, or expert assets can give important direction, viewpoint, and solace. Steady connections advise us that we are not characterized by our battles and that recuperating is conceivable with the assistance of others.

Rediscovering Yourself: Giving up makes space for fresh starts, offering a valuable chance to rediscover what our identity is and the main thing to us. It's an opportunity to reconnect with our interests, interests, and values, liberated from the imperatives of the past. Rediscovering ourselves includes investigating our assets, shortcomings, and goals, embracing the excursion of self-disclosure with interest and receptiveness.

Rehearsing Pardoning: Pardoning is a groundbreaking demonstration that frees us from the shackles of hatred and sharpness. Giving up includes pardoning ourselves as well as other people for past damages, errors, and double-crossings. Pardoning doesn't pardon or support unsafe way of behaving yet rather liberates us from conveying the heaviness of outrage and disdain. Through absolution, we discharge the past and account for adoration, recuperating, and development.

Embracing Development: At its pith, giving up is a course of development and reestablishment. It's tied in with perceiving that endings make ready for fresh starts and that each misfortune contains the seeds of chance. Embracing development implies embracing change, vulnerability, and distress with mental fortitude and flexibility. It's a demonstration of the human soul's ability for change and transformation, advising us that we are equipped for rising like a phoenix after our past to make a more brilliant, really satisfying future. Conclusion: Giving up is difficult, nor is it generally clear. It's a chaotic, convoluted process that requests persistence, boldness, and self-sympathy. However, inside the profundities of giving up lies the commitment of recharging, recuperating, and development. By embracing the groundbreaking force of giving up and pushing ahead with open hearts and brains, we can recover our organization, rediscover our validness, and make a day-to-day existence loaded up with reason, bliss, and significance.

www.ingramcontent.com/pod-product-compliance
Lightning Source LLC
Chambersburg PA
CBHW070755250726
48662CB00004B/1821